MW00900568

The Stinkie Winkie Adventure

"The New Arrival"

Tangee Marcia Dingle

Outskirts Press, Inc.
http://www.outskirtspress.com

ISBN: 978-1-9772-4313-3

Illustrations by Ananda Graham.

Outskirts Press and the "OP" logo are trademarks belonging to Outskirts Press, Inc.

PRINTED IN THE UNITED STATES OF AMERICA

This Book Belongs to:

NOOTZ IS COMING!

It was a good day in the Stinkie Winkie house. Momma Winkie was having a baby! In a few days the Nootz will be here.

Everyone was excited except Roncil. He didn't want a new baby! Him being the baby forever was just fine!

Why did they need a new baby anyway? He was all the baby this family needed. Shoot! This wasn't fair and he was going to make his case known to somebody!

"Momma Winkie, why do we need a new baby? Don't you love me anymore?" said Roncil. Momma scooped him up and smiled at him.

"Of course I do. What would make you say something like that?" Roncil looked around the room and then back at Momma Winkie. "If we get a new baby, what will you do with me?" Momma Winkie said quite frankly, 'where is Novana and Remchi?'

"Well, they're right here in the house with us!" Roncil said. "Exactly!" exclaimed Momma Winkie. "I don't understand Momma Winkie." Roncil said. She explained, if Novana is still here after Remchi was born, that means that I did not get rid of her.

And if Remchi is still here after you were born, then that means that I did not get rid of him. So once Nootz is born what do you think that means? Roncil slowly muttered, "That you won't get rid of me?" Momma Winkie squeezed him and said, 'correct! You'll have to stay right here with us! We hope you don't mind?"

"I sure don't!" Roncil jumped up and down and ran into the Nootz' nursery. "Poppa Winkie, can I help you put the crib together and paint the room for Nootz?"

"You sure Can. Let me guess. You spoke to Momma Winkie about what was going to happen to you once the Nootz arrived and she told you that you were going to stay right here with us?"

"Yup!" Roncil said. I can't wait for the Nootz to get here. I'm going to show her how to fish, hunt and shoot a sling shot!" Roncil was now ready for his new sister. He wasn't afraid of being left out or abandoned when she arrived. Now Roncil knows that just because a mother has a new baby, it doesn't mean that she cannot love them all!

The Nootz arrived two days later and the Stinkie Winkie family couldn't be happier!

Welcome Home Nootz!

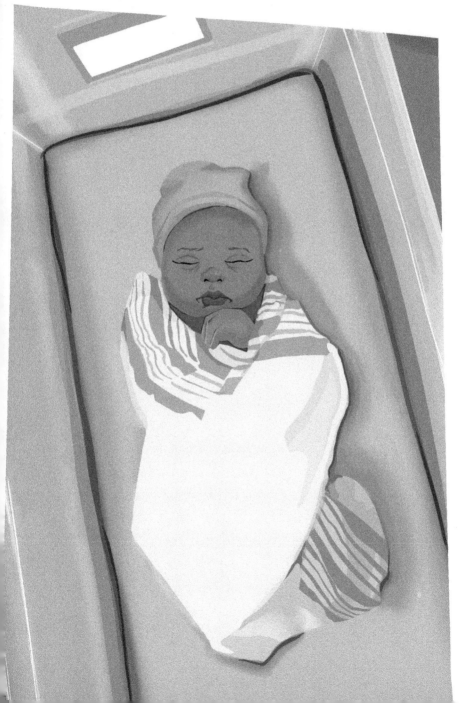

CPSIA information can be obtained
at www.ICGtesting.com
Printed in the USA
BVHW021517210621
610125BV00010B/2660

9 781977 243133